Soar

30 days of rising above

Soar

30 days of rising above

SIMCHA NATAN

simchanatan.com

fb.com/simchanatan
IG: @simchanatan

Soar *30 Days of Rising Above*. © Simcha Natan 2019

ISBN: 978-1-9160597-3-3

Cover illustration by Joe Hateley © Simcha Natan

Design and layout © HerebyDesign

Edited by Abbie Robson

The right of Name to be identified as the author of
this work has been asserted by her/him in accordance with the
Copyright, Designs and Patents Act 1988.

Contents

Introduction	11
Awakened - now what?	12
The power of "I don't know"	14
Constancy	16
Thermals	18
Rising above	20
Isolation	22
Clarity	24
Vistas	26
Thinner oxygen	28
Legacy 2.0	30
Above the story	32
Echoes	34
Vulnerability is strength	36
The crushing	38
Deep wells	40
Mountains and ants	42
Depths and heights	44
Bigger and smaller	46
White flag	48
Battle scars	50

The value of fruit	52
The sudden	54
Wildfire	56
No regret	58
Adventure	60
Perspective	62
Landscape	64
Clouds breaking	66
The strategy	68
Vision	70
Reviews of Dare to Ask	72

Contents

Introduction

$\mathcal{W}$elcome to the third and final part of this *Dare to Ask* adventure! I'm beyond excited to walk through this 30-day experience of learning to *Soar* above it all, and all that that means once we have been awakened to who God is, who we are, and the dreams and callings that God has placed within us.

This devotional brings the adventure of 'daring to ask' full circle. We started our adventure by learning to dream with God again, allowing ourselves to be like little kids as we view our inner passions, desires and drives. This led us to being 'Awakened' to the truth and reality of who God is, and therefore who we are. Through a beautiful process of understanding that none of those dreams and drives were put there accidentally, we have come to see that God has so much more for us!

Now we arrive at this final part of the adventure, where we must learn to Soar with him. We cannot muscle our way through life, even when we understand the purpose and call on our lives; we must learn the peace that passes understanding, a constancy and rest that allows us to rise above while still wrestling for more from God. This is a place of vision and awe that drives us right back to where we started - on our knees! My hope and prayer for you is that, through being awakened, you catch those thermals and soar on wings like eagles!

~ Simcha x

About Dare to Ask

The *Dare to Ask* project is comprised of the umbrella book *Dare to Ask*, which tells the stories and lessons behind songs written in a long season of being hidden. It then takes a more detailed look at the process of daring to ask, starting with the first EP and its counterpart devotional - *Dreaming - 30 days of Dreaming with God*, followed by the second EP and its counterpart devotional - *Awakened - 30 days of waking up and stepping out*. This is the third and final EP and counterpart devotional, *Soar - 30 Days of Rising Above*. Watercolour artwork and calligraphy pieces are available to accompany all parts of the project.

DAY 1

Awakened - now what?

*In their hearts humans plan their course, but the
LORD establishes their steps.
Proverbs 16:9*

*O*nce we have been 'awakened' to who God is, it impacts how
we understand who we are. We realise there was purpose in why
God made us the way we are, the gifts and drives he puts in us,
and the dreams we carry in our hearts. We become alive in a new,
fresh way, a 'bursting with life' way! But then what?

We shouldn't expect to be able to maintain this newly Awakened
state in our own strength. The point of this devotional is to find
how our new perspective leads us to be even more dependent
and in need of God's ability to keep us ascending, to become
more aware and more awakened to him and who he's made us
to be.

This process of learning to *Soar* is one which takes us to unexpected
places, in a sometimes surprising direction. It's important for us
to know that God isn't interested in us 'arriving'. The aim isn't for
us to learn to do this life alone, to outgrow our dependence on
him. While our growth may look like we're getting stuff figured
out and maturing, we should actually be maturing into greater
dependence. It's another principle that goes against that of the

world. In the Kingdom, the more we learn the more we need, the more we seek, the more we press in, the more we depend on Him.

While the world may celebrate independence, success on our own, man-made strength and self provision, God is looking for greater dependence on him, the glory going to him, and our strength being found only in him. He wants to provide for us.

During the process of being awakened, there is a great temptation to think we have 'arrived' and made it! We suddenly get it, we realise why we've had these passions and dreams, and have reconnected with God and understood who he is in a fresh a new way! The temptation is to run from there and try to muster up and maintain this excitement, trying to make decisions based on our new understanding rather than God's spoken guidance. We try to keep this new found excitement in life, but instead of running back to being hidden in him, we think we'll move forwards and learn more by throwing ourselves out there. But the Kingdom of God is always the opposite to the world!

Learning to 'soar' is another example of running towards what the world tells you to avoid.

Are you ready?

Day 2

The power of "I don't know"

*What is mankind that you are mindful of them,
human beings that you care for them?
Psalm 8:4*

There is power in knowing our limits and not being afraid of them. One of the things that happened to me when I went through my own awakening was that I became more aware of how little I know, and how different people are from one other. While coming to a new understanding of what being 'alive' means, I was also overwhelmed by the feeling of being so very small. This wasn't a form of false humility, it was realising just how huge God's creation is and how diverse humanity is, which tends to make me suddenly feel very small!

There are 3 words I have come to understand can dramatically transform the atmosphere of a conversation: "I don't know."

I don't think we don't use them enough. We think we have it all sussed. We've read up on it, we've studied it, we have a degree in it, we've experienced it, we've written a thesis on it, we're an expert in it. These days, if we've checked up on Dr. Google and seen an Instagram post on something, we can see ourselves as a voice of authority on it, but actually, all that we've done is form an opinion. It's not fact.

The power of "I don't know"

I think we need to be more willing to throw up our hands and say "You know what, I don't know!". It gives space to others to be real about where they're at and invites conversation. There is a beauty in the humility it takes to say "I don't know" that allows others to be weak, and have chance to figure their own struggles out.

One of the first lessons in learning to 'soar' is that shift in perspective where we see that we're part of such a big picture. While God is awesome enough to know all the details of our lives, we need to develop humility and become people who set an environment that accepts weakness when the world encourages false strength. I'm a big believer in needing to give ourselves permission to be weak. To process, pray and proceed is something we all need to do.

But this journey isn't just about me and my own walk, it's about my impact on those around me. Am I a life breather, or a life sucker? Am I a person who tops others up, or do I drain them? Am I a person who encourages or pulls down? Do I intimidate or give space to others to shine? Being real with our own weaknesses and creating an environment of humility is a place where others will flourish, because they won't feel threatened by the impression we're trying to give. Instead, they will be attracted to the safe place we create.

Take some time today to look more closely at the environment that we set when we walk into a room. Do we make space for ourselves and others to say, "I don't know?"

Day 3

Constancy

*The counsel of the LORD stands forever, The plans of
His heart from generation to generation.
Psalm 33:11*

*For I, the LORD, do not change
Malachi 3:6*

We touched on the topic of consistency in the second devotional, *Awakened*, noting that it comes with maturity. We are so often 'roller coaster believers', waiting for our next 'high' with God, while experiencing lows, and valleys which affect us so much. We equal the 'highs' with feeling close to God, and lows with God being far away. But I have learned that the aim isn't to end up on a constant high with God. That spiritual 'high' we get from a worship night or conference doesn't necessarily mean that God is closer. It means you walked into a setting where his presence was being welcomed (hopefully!) and your spirit responded to it.

This adventure is all about finding a place in God where there is a constancy. A place where we live in his presence, rather than chasing events in order to find it. It's about understanding that there is no need to keep flapping about trying to find some space to really fly, when we can learn to soar above, resting on the currents on which he carries us, those that allow us to remain at peace, sustaining the walk and giving us longevity.

At the end of *Awakened*, we spoke about birds learning to fly, and the learning process that they go through; being kicked out of the nest by their parents, and helplessly flapping about as they figure out their ability and destiny.

What starts out as a pathetic flapping motion soon becomes second nature. They don't need to attend seminars, conferences, classes and meetings in order to realise that they have this ability; their ability to ride the currents and fly high is something they do every day, as second nature.

There is a place where we can learn to operate that is unshakeable. It's an unchangeable, immovable rock where we can stand firm, no matter what storms may throw at us. It sounds strange, to talk about standing on rocks in the same sentence as flying, but the two do go hand in hand.

It is possible to find this constant life of unwavering truth, in which we have mastered the skill of rising above. We can learn to flip our thinking about things on its head, understanding that the principles of the world are in direct opposition to those of the Kingdom. In that world we can stand on a rock AND soar on a current, no problem!

I was really challenged by this combination – how about you? How do we wake and rise, and yet stand firm, to find that second nature constancy in God? Today, try and think of ways you can rest on the currents and stand on the rock.

DAY 4

Thermals

I lift up my eyes to the mountains—where does my help come from?

Psalm 121:1

Thermals are a natural phenomenon created by hot air from the earth's surface rising up and becoming less dense than the air around it. The lighter air rises and cools as it ascends. It stops when it has cooled to the same temperature as the surrounding air.

We know that eagles love to soar, we've all heard that they ride the thermals, but it can help to understand what those thermals are, how they're made and how we can apply those principles to our own lives.

It is interesting that things 'getting heated' at ground level is what creates perfect conditions for soaring. Our natural response when walking through a heated situation, would be to collapse on the floor and stay close to the situation. We attend to the details, keep an eye on things, and just 'get through' until things cool off. Isn't this how most of us engage with our lives?

Ground level heating up creates an opportunity for choice. We can stay on the ground, keeping our eyes on our steps ahead, on the heated situation, the immediate and the consuming, or we

18

can allow this set of circumstances to elevate us, teach us and carry us.

It is important at this point of the *Dare to Ask* adventure that we understand that these ways of thinking and approaching life are contrary to the world. The more we dig into this process, the more we should see that the ways of the world are contrary to the Kingdom of God. And the closer we walk to God and the more surrendered to him we grow, the more contrary our choices will be come.

Our circumstances can often feel like we're walking through the fire, and we feel beaten, defeated and drained. We fix our gaze on the problem, on finding solutions, on surviving. We don't naturally look at this season in life as an opportunity to find freedom we've not experienced before, to look up and find clarity, and effortlessly glide.

This is the challenge not only for today, but of this whole devotional.

We know God can use the storm we are asking to be rescued from as our rescue, but this concept of soaring is another level from there. Am I willing to rise above the situation? To allow God to use the 'heat' of the situation to provide the means to find new heights above?

DAY 5

Rising above

*Consider it pure joy, my brothers and sisters,
whenever you face trials of many kinds, because
you know that the testing of your faith produces
perseverance.*

James 1:2-3

The notion of 'rising above' is not one of superiority, or greater spirituality. It is one of surrender. It is one of trust, and of letting go.

We learned in the *Awakened* devotional that sometimes the circumstances we're fighting against have been given to us by God as his rescue plan. But even if we have come to accept that we must walk through these circumstances, it's hard to find peace, clarity, vision or refreshment in the storm.

We are conditioned by the world to be unafraid of telling people that we are struggling or suffering. We encourage openness and honesty about where we are at. I have no problem with this, unless it leads to a victim mentality. The two can go hand in hand - we acknowledge that we're struggling, the world congratulates us on our willingness to share, and we are given a free pass to self-pity, playing the victim and collecting sympathy from those around us. This cycle encourages us to stay there, so much so that we no longer know who we are without the struggle. It becomes part of who we are, and a burden. We try to fly with it, but it will eventually ground us and prevent us from being able to rise up.

I do not believe this cycle reflects the values of the Kingdom. Our verse for the day does not line up with victim-hood. I believe that we must arrive at a place where our trials, fires, difficulties, and heated situations lead to greater release, peace, joy and rest.

As we saw in yesterday's devotional, thermals - the perfect conditions for resting and soaring above - are created by heat. And yet we tend to take the human route - looking down on the fire below. We use up energy with our aimless flapping; our direction isn't intentional because we're staring down on the situation below, flying desperately close to the flames, because that's where we feel most in control.

What we haven't understood is that this heat is intended to elevate us to a place of rest where we can look ahead, and find direction, clarity and vision. In God's natural order, heat has been created to rise upwards.

So, are there any victim mentalities that we need to acknowledge and no longer entertain? Think today about whether you have been moving through life without direction, focusing on problems instead of using them as an opportunity to rise above and see new perspectives.

Day 6

Isolation

Whoever dwells in the shelter of the Most High will
rest in the shadow of the Almighty.
Psalm 91:1

$\mathcal{I}$ am a big believer in community and 'doing life' with others in a way that spurs on and encourages. But the concept of sharing everything with everyone is one that I struggle with, because it makes our suffering a community event.

There are times when this is necessary, and helpful, and I would in no way wish to discourage this. However, there is a danger that it could welcome the kind of support that encourages us to dwell on the struggle and remain there. Somehow the kindness, help, love and sympathy start to outweigh the difficulty of the struggle. We choose to remain there for much longer than we need to, because let's face it, we like the attention. I would even go as far as to say that for some of us, we lose sight of who we are without our suffering, and it begins to define who we are.

The interesting thing about soaring on thermals is that it cannot be a community event. The bird cannot be placed on the thermals by others. It cannot find that place of gliding effortlessly above by others putting it there; it needs to do it alone. It has to make a decision to rise above, to let go, to be carried by the current.

Isolation

Finally, the bird can see the bigger picture. It's a place of fresher cleaner air; and it's a place of isolation.

We don't tend to like the concept of isolation. We think it must equal lonely, abandoned and forsaken. But there is safety in the solitude. It is in the isolation that we find where and to whom we truly belong. The isolation of riding the thermals is one of deep trust and surrender, especially after being kicked out of the nest repeatedly in order to learn how to fly in the first place! But it is in the bird's nature to allow that thermal to carry it high above, where it can sit there, wings spread open, carried by the heated air of the situation below.

I believe this is a principle that we can learn from. Everything in our nature wants to go the way the world suggests is best - focusing on the problem situation. We want to know that our problem is seen as valid, and that our victim status is affirmed. We sit in self-pity and allow the circumstance to be sovereign over us.

But maybe God wants us to take our situation not to the public place, but to the secret place; to focus on him, not it, and to find our support, our identity, our joy and our peace in him, rather than our support network. Maybe we shouldn't be looking to validate our victim status, as much as our status as a child of God. Maybe we need to allow the isolation to be the place of safety, perspective and clarity.

Decide today not to despise the quiet, isolated places, but rather to expect to find God in them.

Day 7

Clarity

*For God has not given us a spirit of fear, but of power
and of love and of a sound mind.
2 Timothy 1:7 (NKJV)*

Clarity is something that we often pray for, wait for and seek. A clear and sound mind is something that is connected to boldness. The only way to not be timid, is to be bold. When we walk in boldness we have the promise of a sound mind.

Sometimes, during our ascent on those thermals, we travel through layers of fog. Just like when a road goes up through the clouds, we can feel engulfed, unable to perceive depth or see where we are. It is OK for us to go through times like this. It doesn't mean we don't have a sound mind, it is just part of the process of gaining clarity.

Consider an aeroplane. As it ascends it goes through a large bank of cloud, but once that plane pushes through the tops of those clouds, we have the best clarity we've had. The fog lifts and we see the horizon, the sun, the clouds for what they really are - a temporary fog which lifts when we persevere.

I believe in pushing through and pressing on, continuing towards the last directive we've been given by God, even when our head may feel like it's in a fog. Sometimes that fog is there to test us, sometimes it's there to confuse us, sometimes it's there to intimidate us. But let's go back to that plane - what would happen if that pilot freaked out and stopped piloting every time he went through cloud and couldn't see? The plane would plummet, loose direction, and bring great risk to those on board, as well as delay the arrival at the destination.

We must keep going. We will always encounter those layers of fog, but we will also come through them, and find the greatest clarity. After the fog, the sun is always out! It takes boldness, perseverance and bravery to press on through even when the way ahead isn't clear or obvious.

That is what today is about. Walking out with the boldness that God has promised us will lead to clarity, and we'll begin to understand the roads we've travelled, even if we don't fully grasp it right now. Trust the last directive you were given, and press on towards the goal. The currents will find you, and you will reach soaring altitude!

Take some time today to make sure you know what your last 'orders' were from God, and commit to completing the assignment. He won't give us new tasks until the current one is complete!

DAY 8

Vistas

"Enter through the narrow gate. For wide is the gate and broad is the road that leads to destruction, and many enter through it. But small is the gate and narrow the road that leads to life, and only a few find it."
Matthew 7:13-14

I seek you with all my heart; do not let me stray from your commands.
Psalm 119:10

When I imagine flying, soaring high, I imagine views that stretch out all around, and one of the words that sprung to mind was 'Vista' - so I looked it up.

There are two definitions of the word vista. It's not just a pretty view, it's a view 'seen through a long narrow opening'. When I read this I was blown away. There is so much in the bible about the 'narrow path' of walking with God. Isn't it fitting that our view on things should also be seen through this narrow opening?

This definition of 'vista' was so beautiful. Just imagine looking out through a turret window - you see a whole view, but you're protected. You're informed about your surroundings, but you're not exposed. Our view of our circumstances and season we're in shouldn't be getting wider and broader and more watered down, it should be getting more focused by the Word. We shouldn't expose ourselves to arrows that can be fired at us by views and positions that don't align with the bible. We should remain firm, willing to learn new things which are in line with scripture, while looking out on our vista with our eyes set on the prize.

The second definition of a vista is: 'a mental view of a succession of remembered or anticipated events.' This is a beautiful addition to the concept and understanding of a vista. While looking out over our life, season and surroundings, through this narrow, protected opening, we must remain aware of how far he's brought us. We must remember the things that he's done for us, and remember our first love.

I love this balance between the fullness of the full picture of hindsight, alongside the more narrow revelation of what is to come. We never see the full picture ahead, but we do have the fullness of understanding all that he has done for us by looking back over our lives. This gives us a beautiful peace. We can trust that we don't need the full vista, and that God trusts us with what we need to know, when we need to know it.

Take time today to appreciate the fullness of the hindsight of God's goodness to us, and to intentionally trust in him with the limited vista ahead that we have.

DAY 9

Thinner Oxygen

God is our refuge and strength, an ever-present help in trouble.

Psalm 46:1

So do not fear, for I am with you; do not be dismayed, for I am your God. I will strengthen you and help you; I will uphold you with my righteous right hand.

Isaiah 41:10

It's important in our journey that we don't expect perfection. We need to rise above, and learn this rest that carries us above the storms. On top of that, we need to learn to keep our mind in a place of clarity and truth, fixing our eyes on a heavenly rather than earthly view. But we also need to allow ourselves to have those days where we just can't seem to lift our own heads, let alone fly up onto those thermals.

Developing the habit of soaring doesn't mean we're no longer human, and it's important that we don't punish ourselves for having days in which we struggle more than others. What we cannot allow is the wallowing in that place, allowing the swamp to engulf us so we cannot hear or see truth anymore.

The more we soar with God, and learn to rise above, the higher he will take us and the greater vistas he will show us. But we must remember that the higher we go, the thinner the oxygen is. Above the clouds is a more demanding place physically, and our bodies need to be trained for this. In training for high altitudes, the body will have times when it struggles to feel its best. It takes energy to perform at its peak, and will need moments to recover. It's the same spiritually.

It is a learning process to rise above and go to new heights with God. We are putting our spiritual 'body' through a rigorous regime and it is only natural to have those moments when we feel like we're failing. But I believe these moments prove the exact opposite. In those moments we have a choice. We can give up, walk away and sink into a black hole of self-pity and despair, or we can choose to understand what is happening.

Sometimes we reach the end of the thermal we are on. In that situation we may have to use our training to flap our wings, feed our momentum and find the next thermal. We do not need to plummet to our death; if we are committed to soaring above, we just need to fuel our ascent a little more today!

Even in writing this day of devotional, this is the exact day I am experiencing! I am faced with the choice of despair, desperation and ultimately depression, or I can make a choice to feed myself, choose the life and truth of God, and choose joy.

When the oxygen is thinner, we just need some extra spiritual calories to help our 'body' keep performing. It's not a failure; nothing has gone wrong. It's just part of the training. Take time today to listen to God saying "Come on!! Come higher with me! Feed yourself and you can make it!"

DAY 10

Legacy 2.0

So Jacob was left alone, and a man wrestled with him till daybreak. When the man saw that he could not overpower him, he touched the socket of Jacob's hip so that his hip was wrenched as he wrestled with the man. Then the man said, "Let me go, for it is daybreak."

But Jacob replied, "I will not let you go unless you bless me."

Genesis 32: 24–26

Today is a day for praying big prayers. We have talked a little in previous devotionals about it never being too early to start leaving a legacy. But surely it's not only about leaving something behind us, or inspiring others around us, or pointing to God? What about our own legacy and inheritance?

When Jacob wrestled with the angel, he'd already been given the birthright. So why was he asking for more?

In the story of Jacob and his mother Rebekah in Genesis 27, I believe that Rebekah knew that her son's birthright was meaningless and incomplete if it did not have the seal of blessing from the one who bestowed it. He had to receive the Father's blessing for the birthright to become manifest.

Jacob was an obedient son. He did as his mother instructed him, and as far as we can tell, he did it without question, even though he must have understood the scale of 'trickery' his mother was asking of him. Somehow, however, Rebekah knew that Jacob was the son that God intended to carry the legacy that had been promised to her husband Isaac, and father-in-law, Abraham. When Esau showed such disregard for this inheritance, trading it for a mere bowl of soul, she must have felt justified!

Fastforward years later to Genesis 32 - Jacob had received an unexpected inheritance; he was walking in an undeserved blessing, yet still he picked a fight with God for more! It's a very real and raw moment between the angel and Jacob. Here, he was given a new name - the name that means 'struggle'. In that moment he was touched, and marked in a way that made him never the same again.

Our legacy isn't only about what we leave behind for others, it's about stepping into the fullness and blessing of ALL that God has given US, and being willing to contend with God for more. It may be a struggle, it may be uncomfortable, it may mark us so that we're never the same again - but that is the place where we see God face to face. It's the place where transformation happens, perspective gained, and authority is given.

Maybe you have already stepped into your inheritance and have already been blessed, but you can always ask God to enlarge your territory. Just be prepared that he may need to do some work on you in order for you to handle the enlarged territory he has for you!

DAY 11

Above the storm

The LORD said, "Go out and stand on the mountain in the presence of the LORD, for the Lord is about to pass by." Then a great and powerful wind tore the mountains apart and shattered the rocks before the Lord, but the Lord was not in the wind.

After the wind there was an earthquake, but the Lord was not in the earthquake.

After the earthquake came a fire, but the Lord was not in the fire. And after the fire came a gentle whisper.

1 Kings 19: 11-12

When Elijah saw the glory of God, he had climbed up a mountain. He had separated himself from everyday life, and ascended to a high place. We all know the conversation that followed: God wasn't in the wind, or the fire, or the earthquake, but in the gentle whisper.

The still, small voice is not a new concept to us, but we must incline our ear to hear. It's not something that we can hear above the noise and crashing of daily life.

I have come to realise that this place is not somewhere you can find by just locking yourself away from whatever is outside.

When you're in a storm, whether it be a hurricane, an earthquake or a fire, the only places you can find perfect peace are in the eye of the storm, or by rising above the storm clouds.

This means pushing to the centre of the storm, allowing the heat of the fire to carry us on those thermals, and finding that immovable rock in the middle of the earthquake.

We spoke earlier about how thermals that carry eagles are created by hot air rising; here we see the application of it. In all three of these examples, there is significant heat involved in the situation. Hurricanes, fires and earthquakes all need heat or friction in order to occur.

I love it when nature leads the way, showing us the beautiful simplicity of God's plan!

Just as birds need hot air rising to be lifted to the current that carries them, so we also need to be lifted above the storms we are in. Only then can we find peace and clarity and truly hear the voice of God. That whisper is carried on the thinner air, high above it all, if we can only rise up on those thermals, and soar above the storms.

Take time today to quieten your soul enough to hear that still small voice. Commit to the idea of God wanting you to rise above and not focus on the storm, and let him carry you above and show you new things. This may reveal things about your own character, about the situation you're in or about the people around you that you never would have seen or learned had you not entered the storm. The key is to train your ear to hear that still small voice.

DAY 12

Echoes

"I the LORD do not change..."

Malachi 3:6

Jesus [Messiah] is the same yesterday and today and forever.

Hebrews 13:8

I believe God's voice does several things. Firstly, his voice always creates. It always speaks life. It gives power and authority and can turn the world upside down. I believe there are times that God's voice can pierce through a situation, cutting right across what we are doing so that everything changes in an instant. But I also believe that God's voice echoes through eternity with truths that never change. These are the things we should always be led by and should cling to as our identity and security in a world that is trying to stick so many other 'truths' to us.

Because he is always creating, and his voice is a creative force, our very beings reverberate with his heartbeat. Those simple eternal truths are never undone, never changed. Not a syllable he speaks is wasted. The breath of God that created humanity stretches through all of time and reaches into our own situations to bring life, hope and healing.

Those echoes of eternity should be our anchor. They should tether us to truth and give us identity, value and security. They should permeate our beings in a way that nothing else can, because they are both in our very DNA as a creation of our creator, and all around us, because they are part of the very nature of God.

There is safety in this echo because what God says through time, what he utters and the breath he exhales, is never wasted. It's never unintentional and it's always on time. These are the things we can rest in, build on and stand firm in.

Yesterday we studied the still small voice; this IS the echo we are discussing today. We find this unexpectedly small voice, from a big God, when we rise above the noise of life. When we accept that the heat of our situation is what will teach us the art of ascending, we discover an atmosphere that is perfect for hearing the voice of God in a way we aren't able to anywhere else.

Today is a day for committing to truths and making sure we're anchored in the right things. Make sure you know God's truth from his Word and have spoken it over any stormy situations in your life, and rest in the peace of all his echoes through time, which are the same today as ever.

Day 13

Vulnerability is strength

"My grace is sufficient for you, for my power is made perfect in weakness." Therefore I will boast all the more gladly about my weaknesses, so that [Messiah]'s power may rest on me. That is why [...] I delight in weaknesses, in insults, in hardships, in persecutions, in difficulties. For when I am weak, then I am strong.

2 Corinthians 12:9–10

I have often been told one of my 'flaws' is trusting people too easily, and that I'm too open with my heart - in other words, I live in a state of vulnerability. We are taught that vulnerability is risky and should be avoided. For many years, I tried to fight my vulnerable nature, convinced that it was going to get me hurt - many times, it did. However, I realise now that in the process, I had deliberately turned my heart of flesh into a heart of stone. In fact, undoing this hardening was far more painful than the hurt I'd experienced through my vulnerability.

It took years to walk through the painful process of unfreezing my heart. I have now come to see how vulnerability is one of the gifts that God has given me, and have begun to embrace it and all that comes with it - including the hurt. I've discovered that my own vulnerability makes others feel welcomed and accepted; they can feel safe, at home and loved. I have witnessed that this vulnerability can carry incredible strength.

Rather than seeing someone else's vulnerability as an opportunity to feel better about ourselves, it takes strength to lay down our own personal layers of protection and be vulnerable also.

Because actually, it is when we are vulnerable that we are our most real, true, naked selves, closest to God's original design for us.

Perhaps the most important thing about vulnerability is that it involves surrender. We must surrender our pride, our strength and our self made ability. God is always looking for fully surrendered hearts, they are his prized possession! Why? Because surrendered hearts don't try to steal his glory! They increase it!

We must also not forget to also make ourselves vulnerable before God. Our verse for today talks about boasting in our weaknesses. Being vulnerable may feel like a place of weakness, but it is actually a place of courage, of choice and of incredible healing and refreshment. Remember, our weaknesses are his opportunities! It's where the truth is faced and accepted, and love is exchanged. It's the place we learn how to operate in his strength and his love, where our fallen human nature fails.

Commit today to being real and vulnerable before God, even if you don't have a person to do this with. There is a beauty in unmasking ourselves before God, because our masks never fooled him in the first place! He can work far more with a person who is willingly weak before him, than someone who hasn't learned where the mask ends and the person begins.

DAY 14

The crushing

Now it is God who makes both us and you stand firm in [Messiah]. He anointed us, set his seal of ownership on us, and put his Spirit in our hearts as a deposit, guaranteeing what is to come.

2 Corinthians 1:21-22

Raw is a very popular term these days - raw diet, raw ingredients, raw make up. Eating natural and unaltered food has definitely been proven to lead to a healthier diet.

God has a beautiful way of teaching us eternal truths through his creation, law and methods. We have spoken before, in the book *Dare to Ask,* about the process of making pure oil, but there is still more to be learned from the olive press.

In order for oil to come forth, an olive must go through a dark season when it is being crushed by a huge millstone. The produce of the first harvest, the initial squeeze of a batch is set aside as anointing oil. It is in the crushing that anointing is found.

When we are crushed and squeezed, there is less of us. We are poured out, broken, like a hollow shell of a previously lush fruit. We may feel completely undone by a storm from which we've been unable to escape. But **this** is the place where God can step in, fill us up and anoint us. It is only through the olive's crushing of the olive, that the anointing oil pours forth.

I would suggest that we may not constantly live in a special state of 'anointing'. We have gifts that God has given us, which we should invest in, practice and make sharp, ready for use. But it is when we are poured out, at the end of ourselves, and NOT relying our natural abilities, that God can step in, and truly bring transformation through it. Only when there is nothing of us left in that olive that its purpose is used for anointing.

When we realise these truths, our prayers change significantly. We no longer run away from the difficulties. We no longer beg for mercy from the hardships. We no longer punish ourselves and blame God for everything that's difficult in our lives. Rather, we start to understand that he has called us to walk the same path that he did - one of refining, perfecting and ascending. This is when we receive an anointing from God, when we agree to learn what needs to be learned rather than fighting against his methods. That perfecting process means we can be used by God, and change the room we're in through our surrendered life in his hand.

So today, we need to answer for ourselves this hard question - if I want God's anointing, do I 'dare to ask' for the crushing?

DAY 15

Deep Wells

*Deep calls to deep
in the roar of your waterfalls;*

*all your waves and breakers
have swept over me*

Psalm 42:7

It is during times of crushing that our souls yearn and long most deeply for God. I believe there are depths to our souls which resonate with the depths of eternity. There are places in us which are so deep we cannot describe the longings, and we can't fathom the depths. I believe this is our deep calling out for his deep. These deep longings resonate with eternity, for which we were created.

We try to find what we're looking for in many places, thinking "this is what I was hoping for!" Yet the deep longing of our hearts can only be met in God.

The period of crushing continues until we realise that in order to find contentment, we need to find the deepest wells, the places that provide refreshment, the cool water we can draw long and deep from. We need don't stumble around looking for these, they were there all along - we just don't turn to them.

This well is actually in us, but we choose to fill it with junk, which clog and block the call and response from deep to deep. We throw in unhealthy stuff we've been feasting our eyes upon, things we can't be bothered to deal with, hurts, broken relationships, and bitterness, and then wonder why, when we do turn to the well, it's so bitter to the taste.

I've spoken before about our hearts being like attic rooms filled with junk, where we store so many negative things, rather than treating it like the throne room that it should be. Our soul tells the same story. It should be a place of purity, that God can fill up with himself, bringing all the nourishment we need. But he cannot fill a space that isn't there. Sometimes we grant him a shallow spot to fill up, and we think it's enough, but when we turn to it, it's tepid, cloudy with dust. Drinking from this 'puddle' leaves us unfulfilled.

It's time for us to clear our wells out. Our souls are deep, deep places, which God can fill to overflowing with all that we need to rise above. He can give us the sustenance, nourishment and refreshment that our souls need. But he cannot fill a well that isn't a receptacle.

Once we allow this infilling to happen, we become a source of life to others also. Not that others drink from our well, but because our 'cup runs over', and the refreshment, life and joy that we find, is contagious.

Take some time today to intentionally sort through your heart and soul. They are deep - but what is in them? Have we clogged them up? Thrown trash down there? Are we poisoning our well, so that what comes out is bitter to us and to others?

DAY 16

Mountains and ants

*Come, let us sing for joy to the LORD; let us shout
aloud to the Rock of our salvation. Let us come before
him with thanksgiving and extol him with music and
song. For the LORD is the great God, the great King
above all gods.*

Psalm 95:1-3

Recently God blessed my husband and me with a trip away –
the first we'd had in a decade! We found an incredible deal and
headed to the Dolomite mountains in Northern Italy. When
we arrived in the night, we had no idea what was surrounding
beyond the cute little lights and buildings we could see.

At sunrise, we were both absolutely spellbound by the majesty
and enormity of the mountains that were surrounding us on
all sides, the snow-covered peaks, the pine trees, the dramatic
outline of every rock face that was so unique and full of character.
It was breathtaking. The awe of our surroundings did not wear
off during all the days we stayed there; God knew that this
setting provided soul food for me in a way very few places could.

I gazed for hours at the mountains around me, in awe of the
sheer size of them. God was really showing off when he made
those mountain ranges! But what really blew me away was

watching people skiing and how tiny they looked in comparison. At times they seemed so small that you would barely know they were there.

What hit me in that moment was that God could make these majestic, enormous mountains, and yet be interested in these ant-like humans who were skiing down their slopes.

The inconceivable size of the mountains next to God's attention to detail was so obvious in that moment. He is able to create impressive and imposing mountain ranges around the world. He has created planets, solar systems and an ever-growing universe. Yet the thing that preoccupies him day and night are the thoughts of my mind, the motives of my heart, and our communion together. Those rocks and mountains don't have a relationship with Him, but if I don't praise him, they will cry out in my place.

Today is all about worship. There is something awesome about seeing the magnitude of creation through fresh eyes, whilst at the same time knowing that God wants to meet with me. We should be worshipping him for all he is, for all he's done and for all he will be. Take some time to allow the beauty of creation and character of God overwhelm you to the point of worship, whilst allowing your relationship and communion with him to get closer.

Day 17

Depths and heights

To the roots of the mountains I sank down;
the earth beneath barred me in forever.

But you, Lord my God,
brought my life up from the pit.

Jonah 2:6

I once heard an incredible speaker who said: "The depths of the valleys we walk are in direct correlation to the heights that God wants to take us to" (Graham Cooke).

I remember being impacted by this, as I was walking in a particularly deep, dark valley at the time. I remember being encouraged that this valley might be an indication of where God wanted to take me.

However, as time passed, I learned that I cannot use this as a bargaining chip. A life of surrender doesn't mean that I get to claim my 'heights'. Just because I've done my time in the valleys doesn't mean that I'm now entitled to 'the good life'.

There is a Hollywood mindset that can overtake us as we are convinced that 'our day will come'. We've woven 'making it' or 'success' into a perverted understanding of blessing, when it is really just the epitome of an empty, worldly construct of fame and fortune.

There are some who are called into the world of fame and fortune because that is where God is taking them to partner in his Kingdom. Contrary to popular belief, this isn't an easy world; it is made entirely of plastic and emptiness. And yet it seems to be something we strive for as believers. We want to be known, be seen, feel important, or valued by others. For some reason being known, seen and valued by God is not enough for us.

I have come to understand that these valley seasons are not an indication of the physical height he will take me. They are not a plastic promise of wealth or things 'going my way'. It's a promise of new heights that can be reached with God - new parts of himself that he wants to show me, new aspects of his character that he wants me to represent. It's new ideas and plans that he wants to share and partner in with me.

Rising to heights like eagles is a lonely, isolated place. It's not a crowded room with people cheering you on. You are in a place of solitude that others may never make it to. But it is the place of the greatest perspective, the greatest views, the greatest currents and the greatest blessing.

Take time today to check the heart for any sense of entitlement, or deals you're trying to make with God. Make sure the motives of the heart are pure and pursuing the things God would have for us - not the things of the world.

DAY 18

Bigger and smaller

Humble yourselves, therefore, under God's mighty hand, that he may lift you up in due time. Cast all your anxiety on him because he cares for you.

1 Peter 5:6-7

$\mathcal{I}$ have witnessed great men and women of God find fame in the world's eyes. At the same time I have seen even greater heroes who have served God faithfully in private. The reality is that the size of audience that we are trusted with has no significance at all. God is after the heart that we carry as we serve him.

Whether we serve in secret or in public, on insignificant or large assignments in the world's eyes, God wants us to remain humble before him. He can do incredible things through one person, but the smaller a person recognises themselves to be, the greater the impact they will have for the Kingdom, whether that is affecting one life or many.

In this *Dare to Ask* adventure, there may come moments when we could become puffed up with pride. Perhaps when we realise God has given us our dreams for a reason, or when we understand that he has a unique and instrumental plan for our lives that no one else in history can fulfil. It could be when we have a fresh revelation of who God is, and who he's made us to be, or when we wake up to our partnership in the Kingdom.

There are so many opportunities for us to become proud in the gifts and callings he's given us, rather than seeing them as tools given to fulfil his purpose. We can easily turn our backs on the divine strength we need and lift up our own name rather than glorifying his. But we must constantly remain on bended knee. The higher God takes us, the greater the reach he gives us, the wider our voice travels, the lower we should bow.

God can trust a surrendered life. He can give more to a person who fully understands that they cannot do anything without him. We credit ourselves far too much with human power and ability, and we don't realise that even that is given to us by him.

This isn't a day about famous people – our roles are all different. We each have our sphere that God has ordained us to influence. It doesn't matter the size, shape or location. The point is that God is looking for a fully surrendered life. God can do more through a surrendered life, than a life fighting for its own glory.

We have all been equipped us for what God has ordained for us to do. Sometimes we miss the fullness of what he has for us, because we're too busy focused on someone else's role. Take time today to make sure that you're not striving after someone else's calling.

DAY 19

White flag

For to me, to live is [Messiah] and to die is gain.
Philippians 1:21

"The Lord will fight for you; you need only to be still."
Exodus 14:14

The white flag is well known as a sign of surrender, a signal that a soldier or army had given up and were ready for someone else to take control of the situation. To raise a white flag is to adopt a position of weakness or vulnerability. But since we know that God's Kingdom has opposite principles to the world's, an act of surrender is not as pathetic as the world might have us believe.

We all possess within us a white flag which we can wave at any time, but it is with confidence and intentionality that we can stand and raise our banner of surrender. We need not consider this for a long time, debating the pros and cons. It is a simple transaction. We stand still, and the Lord will fight for us.

When we stand waving our flag, we are exposed to the enemy, and have to consider the risk of attack as we make ourselves visible. When we intentionally surrender to the king, that same action of waving our white flag automatically puts a target on our back for the enemy to attack. A surrendered soul is a danger to the kingdom of darkness. While this shouldn't change our decision as to whether or not we surrender, we must understand that the consequence of our decision is greater attack.

It is in this holy exchange of control, where we give ourselves to him, that the truth of the concept "I count it all as loss" is learned. To win this war we need to fall to our knees, understanding that "to live is Messiah, and to die is to gain".

Sometimes we think far too highly of our abilities. But the sooner we learn that the most effective way for us to partner with God for the kingdom is to surrender, the better! We just we weren't made to do it alone! We need to give it all up, and be crushed and anointed, so we can gain everything in him.

I have had to learn this lesson even through the musical production during this project. I was sick for the vocal recording portion of every single EP. In fact, it became such a trend that by the 3rd EP my production team knew in advance I'd be battling against a hoarse voice! They were right, and I was unable to rely on ability or talent on those days. It was surrender each day to stand at the mic and open my mouth to sing.

Today is all about choosing to be still. It's about surrendering and intentionally stepping down from the fight. You can't do it all – you're not supposed to. God can. Choose to hand over the fight to him, and to watch him fight for you. You need only be still.

Day 20

Battle scars

...being confident of this, that he who began a good work in you will carry it on to completion until the day of [Messiah] Jesus

Philippians 1:6

We so often are ashamed of our scars. We hide them or cover them up, as if they testify to our personal failure. We hope that no one notices them. We learn to talk in such a way that people won't know the real truth - that we've walked through a situation that has left us wounded.

Even in our church culture we often find ourselves striving for perfection - or at least to present the appearance of perfection – especially if we wish to be considered as someone who can lead or be seen 'from the front'.

I believe there is a difference between 'real' and 'raw'. A 'raw' person is going through a private process, where they are still healing. Just like an open wound that should be covered to protect from infection, that needs to be treated and tended to until a scar has developed, while a wound is 'raw' it should not be shared with others widely; it should be a protected time.

A 'real' person has already healed. They may still have scars, but their healing is more complete. It's important to note here, that there is a difference between a scab and a scar. A scab is a protective cover *during* the healing process that can easily get knocked off to re-open the wound, making it vulnerable to infection again. It is only when a wound has fully healed that a person is ready to share their scars to others around them.

I believe that scars can be a wonderful testimony of how far God has brought us. They are a map of his victories, and our partnership with him. They show a log of the discoveries we've made, of who God is, who he's made us to be, the mistakes we've learned from and the obstacles he has overcome through us.

Maybe we weren't always walking hand-in-hand with him, but that doesn't mean he wasn't still fighting for our destiny and our life. Even the scars gained running away from him tell the story of his triumph.

The important thing to realise about scars is that they are healed. They are not open wounds. They are not delicate scabs that could reopen. They are closed and dealt with. Yes - we are marked for life, but if that be the case, we are in good company! Jacob's scars Jacob's scars (Gen. 32:22-32) showed his wrestling match with God had paid off and he'd received his blessing.

We need to make sure that we are operating from a place of 'real' and not sharing our open wounds with the world. Take time today to look at the areas of your life that you share with others, and assess which scars are fully healed, and which may not be. Don't be afraid of sharing fully healed scars with others - they're like a map of your discoveries and God's victories and can bring hope and healing to others who are still raw.

Day 21

The value of the fruit

Am I now trying to win the approval of human beings, or of God? Or am I trying to please people? If I were still trying to please people, I would not be a servant of [Messiah].

Galatians 1:10

Produce fruit in keeping with repentance.

Matthew 3:8

What is your definition of success? Is it Twitter followers? Facebook likes? Wealth? Being the best at something?

I think we all fall into believing wrong definitions of what success is more often than we like to admit. We assume that other people's opinions or approval dictate whether or not something in our lives is a success. But what if the definition of success is simply bearing the fruit which we've been made to bear?

A successful fruit tree isn't bothered about how tall, bushy, pretty or climbable it is. These things may be extra blessings, but its success is actually how fruitful it is and how it nourishes others.

So many of us have wrapped our identity up with our own definition of success. We find our value in a system we've created, and calculate our worth against this counterfeit measuring stick, instead of the heavenly pattern. I meet people all the time who are angry, broken, bitter and in despair because God has not done or given them what they want. But they are basing their value on what they think they should have been, and therefore think very little of themselves. This is not humility, this is a lie.

We need to be secure in our identity in God, rather than looking to outside sources for affirmation, approval and worth. These are fickle, their praises are man-made and not eternal. If we insist on choosing to carry these burdens we will not be able to catch the currents that God has for us.

When we find our identity and worth in the right places, the pressure is off. The words of man do not weigh down or dictate, and our value system and measuring stick changes dramatically!

If we have faithfully done the assignments God has given us to the best of our ability and in partnership with him, then we have succeeded. We may never see earthly fruit, we may never receive the praises of man, we may never be held up as a success by the world's plastic measuring stick. But we will soar, we will be taken to heights that we never could with all that weight on us, we will be shown secrets of heaven because God can trust our hearts. We will encounter the presence of God in ways many never do, because we are only interested in his affirmations and approval.

Take some time today to really assess where you're drawing your value from. Whose voice is affirming you the most? Where do es your identity lie? Identify if your identity has been attacked, claim back the things God has spoken over your life, and start living by them.

Day 22

The sudden

Suddenly a furious storm came up on the lake, so that the waves swept over the boat. But Jesus was sleeping.
Matthew 8:24

God is stronger than me. The strength of his commitment to my best is stronger than my will. He gives me opportunities every day to grow and change into his likeness, but I'm often too locked in on my will to notice them. So God uses other methods to guide me.

I think we like the idea of our nice, neat, little world. We've arranged it so perfectly. But God isn't as bothered about our predictable plans as he is about us living in the fullness of what he has for us. His way may be more risky, more adventurous and more unknown, but it's always a life more alive, more engaged and more released!

When something sudden happens, I have learned to ask, "have I been stubborn?" – and the answer is usually "yes"! The sudden stops us in our tracks. It brings a new perspective and causes us to consider unchartered paths. The sudden makes us open our eyes to new things and forces us to make different choices.

The sudden also brings testing. How will I react? How will I fare in these circumstances? The truth of what is in my heart will come to the surface; my immediate reaction to this situation glares back at me like a reflection in mirror. It becomes clear just how prone to self-pity I am, or where my true motives lie.

The sudden provides an opportunity for us to seek God in a situation and hear what his heart is. Our natural instinct is to fix it, to bulldoze through and to throw a tantrum in self-pity. When we do that, we miss the potential in the new situation - one that God can always use for good.

An example of this came recently when I had saved up to print a full batch of books. When I went to pick them up, we discovered that the whole batch had been corrupted, and weren't sell-able or useable. This was NOT the plan - I was absolutely devastated!

After a few minutes of self-pity (I'm only human!) I remembered how often God asks me to walk through what I am writing about - this was my opportunity to learn to 'rise above'! So, I started asking God what he wanted me to do with these books, these 'rejects' that I had to pay for anyway. All sorts of ideas started to flow that would have never have come to me otherwise, and brought a whole direction that I never would have thought of had the 'rejects' and I never crossed paths!

This may seem like a small situation, but I could have easily indulged it much longer. I didn't have the perfect response immediately, but I'm learning to reposition my heart faster as these things come along. The sudden is usually an indication of my stubbornness, and a wake-up call that I need to consider something differently.

Have you ever been in a season of sudden? What changed for you? Today, can you be brave enough to pray for it again?

DAY 23

Wildfire

… let us offer to God acceptable worship, with reverence and awe, for our God is a consuming fire.
Hebrews 12:28b–29

Wildfire is something we tend to think about negatively. It conjures up images of homes being ravaged, towns being destroyed, firefighters, and out of control blazes. Fire can be seen to be a destructive force of nature, and it can be.

But it can also be a sign of passion. The Bible is full of references to fire. The violence of God's affection towards us and the effect of his presence is compared to mountains melting like wax, and an all-consuming fire. In fact, fire makes the ground more fertile.

We know the rules of pruning for greater fruitfulness, but do we know the rule of fires and fertility? Fire will increase mineralisation rates in soil which increases the fertility of the ground, making it choice ground for new plants and vegetation. It also burns away the leftover vegetation that could suffocate the new growth.

If we apply those principles to our lives, what does that mean?

God's love burns deep in the mystery of a God who breathed

mountains, who can incinerate fears in an instant, and who burns with love towards each human creation he has made. He passionately pursues the depths of who we are, chasing every part of us.

Sometimes God is intentional when it comes to putting us through sudden, fiery seasons. He may want to challenge our fears, or remove things which have been taking our focus. He may want to shed light on something new, redirect us, or simply prepare the ground for receiving something new.

We don't like fire when it's applied to our lives. It's hard, hot and uncomfortable and it brings out the dregs of what is in our hearts. However, this is a perfect climate for our 'soaring' practice. It refines the gold of what we can offer him, and it forces us to choose how we're going to respond. The thermals that form the currents upon which we can ride are being created by the rising heat.

We have a choice: we can hide under a rock and allow the fire to pass by, possibly getting burnt, hurt or choked on fumes, or we can take advantage of the heat that it produces to rise above - finding safety in the heights, knowing that the fire will pass having made our hearts more fertile for new things.

E.M Bounds says, "Prayer ascends by fire. Flame gives prayer access as well as wings, acceptance as well as energy. There is no incense without fire; no prayer without flame."

Today, make a conscious choice to acknowledge this, and allow the fire access to your heart.

DAY 24

No regret

*Or do you show contempt for the riches of his
kindness, forbearance and patience, not realizing that
God's kindness is intended to lead you to repentance?*
Romans 2:4

*The Son is the radiance of God's glory and the exact
representation of his being, sustaining all things by
his powerful word. After he had provided purification
for sins, he sat down at the right hand of the Majesty
in heaven*
Hebrews 1:3

So many of us live a life of regret. We wish that we hadn't
done certain things, or had made different decisions, or that
things hadn't happened the way they did. But living a life of
regret denies that God is sovereign. It denies God's masterful
attention to detail in our lives, and it denies his knowledge of
every intricate occurrence that takes place.

Sometimes God allows things to happen to us, or for us to walk
through things, because he knows what we need to make us
strong, or wise, or courageous. He knows what we need in order
to want, seek and to find him more. He knows what we need to
go through to realise who he's made us to be, what he's placed

within us, and what he's called us to do.

Through regret, we deny God has a plan for us. Regret removes the power from God and credits it to us. It shows that we think we have the power to mess up God's plans for our lives.

There is a difference between regretting specific actions and living in regret. We all make mistakes, but some of us remain in that regret. We haven't learned from those moments and left them in the past, we have allowed them to define us, and our value, to poison the deep wells of our soul.

Do we learn from these mistakes? Or live in them?

When we live in regret, three things are happening. Firstly, we are ignoring that God is forever showing kindness towards us, even though it is it his kindness that leads us to repentance. Secondly, we are rejecting the forgiveness that has been paid for us. We deny the price that the Messiah paid in his sacrifice, and that our transgressions have been removed from us. Lastly, we are choosing to carry around the weight of our mistakes, which keeps us from rising above.

Take time today to cut the ties with any regrets. Leave them in the past and allow the burden to fall away. Give the sovereignty back to God and agree with him to learn from mistakes made, rather than allowing them to define you.

DAY 25

Adventure

Trust in the Lord with all your heart, and lean not on your own understanding; in all your ways submit to him, and he will make your paths straight.
Proverbs 3: 5-6

I will instruct you and teach you in the way you should go; I will counsel you with my loving eye on you.
Psalm 32:8

I'm a firm believer that God is constantly looking for friends to join his adventure. I don't believe that he is up there in heaven, sitting on a huge throne, giving out orders without so much as a glance. He is intricately involved in and inspired by the details of our lives, and has fantastic plans for each of us.

Many of us are locked into a list of things that we believe we need in life, and we won't and don't consider anything outside of that list until our own tasks are accomplished. Reaching a certain level at work, a certain number of children, a certain amount of savings, etc - these things can consume years of our existence.

But what if God is waiting, excited, longing for you to look up and see that there is a life of adventure waiting? A life, filled by challenges, where you can truly see him at work each day?

Adventure

I am convinced that God has tailor-made us for a unique adventure. The challenge today is to identity the reason for the position we're in. If we are working towards our own definition of what we need and cannot move outside of that, then we have missed the point. We have succumbed to the grind of chasing an earthly safety net, but are missing our calling and destiny.

It is valid to seek to meet earthly needs, but we can forget one thing: God doesn't invite us on an adventure and then abandon us. He intends to provide for his children, in exactly the same way we hope we can provide for ours, except he's able to do it in abundance! We can be tempted to settle for our own provision for ourselves, instead of giving God a chance to provide far and beyond what we can even hope for.

If we have a job that we know is serving God's purposes first, even if indirectly, and have passion and vision for why we do what we do each day, then we are on track. That is the adventure. We aren't supposed to live the largest portion of our lives slogging away for someone else, we are supposed to live for our heavenly master, partnering uniquely on a tailor-made journey through this life, for the Kingdom's sake!

There are seasons where we are supposed to serve someone else's vision. Our call might be to be 'under' someone else for a time, where it's not our dreams that we're living, but theirs that we're serving. But even then, this is a calling that we can 'own', like an Elisha, a Jonathan, or a Timothy.

Take some time today to analyse the reasons for your position, and see if there are any adjustments that need to take place.

Day 26

Perspective

When you pass through the waters, I will be with you; and when you pass through the rivers, they will not sweep over you. When you walk through the fire, you will not be burned; the flames will not set you ablaze.

Isaiah 43:2

As we learn how to rise above the situations we are in, it changes our perspective on everything. A grace and peace settles on all that we walk through - no matter the circumstances. It's like walking through the fire and not being burned.

I have experienced this several times, when God has given me an ability to rise above difficult situations that in the natural I know I couldn't do alone. We will all go through seasons that stress us out, drain us and pull us down, and yet we can emerge at the other end refreshed, at peace and filled up.

Once, we were walking through a really tough season as a family, financially, emotionally, and physically. I remember one day that I noticed that even though, humanly speaking, I had license to feel defeated and depressed, yet somehow, God gave me supernatural joy and peace in the midst of it all.

This genuinely concerned me, that maybe I was just numb inside, maybe I should be feeling it all more and feeling weighed down.

But I felt a quiet confidence in my spirit that NO - I had simply been able to rise above the situation and find that peaceful place in the heights.

However, as God helps us to rise above and soar, we must do so in humility. There is strength on offer to fly and soar above it all, yet we shouldn't be boasting of our new found constancy or the stability that we've found in God. This isn't about being more spiritual, more mature, or 'higher' than others in our walk with God. This is simply about living a fully surrendered life, one that is willing to trust the currents no matter what the cost.

When we do this, our perspective on everything changes. No longer do we make deals with God, or ask him for things with a sense of entitlement. We stop taking things for granted, and wave that white flag all over again.

This is a private process, one that comes from praying, processing and progressing onto new and better things. It's not a process that comes from a public, loud voice that puts itself above others. There is no room for pride in a life that wants to soar.

Seek God today and ask him to reveal any pride. Check for any self-taught flying techniques and commit to a life of humble soaring.

DAY 27

Landscape

Believers in humble circumstances ought to take pride in their high position. But the rich should take pride in their humiliation—since they will pass away like a wild flower... Humble yourselves before the Lord, and he will lift you up.
James 1:9-10, 4:10

As we gain higher and higher ground, we learn to read the lay of the land below better. We learn to understand the 'signs of the times' and to hear the whisper of God that is found in that place of solitude. It may be that we hear things that are unpopular when shared. It may be that we see things coming that others cannot see or believe.

The reward for pursuing this place of soaring, is that there is safety in the solitude. There is peace among the heights. There's clarity in the open views, and rest in his mighty presence. These things go against the natural, as does our understanding of the landscape below and what is ahead.

The important thing to keep in mind on this adventure is that no one ever said it would be easy - but it will be blessed. What God can do with a surrendered life that is subjected to his purifying voice can turn the world upside down, and we will see and hear things from God that we can't imagine.

Remember that God isn't interested in our temporary happiness, but in our eternal character, so if things are a little hard, think about the character upgrade you're receiving!

- ≈ Don't be afraid of being alone. You'll find all you need in him.
- ≈ Don't be afraid of not being believed. You'll see the fruit of your surrender in the blessing on your life.
- ≈ Don't be afraid of the high places. You will find greater perspective and understanding from those places.
- ≈ Don't be afraid of losing your way. You will find new ground that you would never have seen if you hadn't risen so high.

Remember - the depths you walk mirror the heights you'll fly. The higher he takes us, the lower we should bow. Take some time today to think about the depths you may have walked, the fears you may be carrying and exchange them for the promise of heights and perspective.

Day 28

Clouds breaking

Their work will be shown for what it is, because the Day will bring it to light. It will be revealed with fire, and the fire will test the quality of each person's work.
1 Corinthians 3:13

For there is nothing hidden that will not be disclosed, and nothing concealed that will not be known or brought out into the open.
Luke 8:17

When we think of clouds breaking, we often imagine it as a break in the storm - the sun shines through a break in the clouds and it's a little bit of light relief. Things are revealed that couldn't be seen before.

When the clouds break, both the birds who soar and those below see things that they couldn't see before. Likewise, as we look up towards the light, we see these birds flying above it all which we hadn't been aware of before. We all get to see the lay of the land below and sky above in a new way.

It is impossible to keep things hidden from God - there is nothing that won't eventually be revealed. The clouds breaking allows light not only to shine onto what lies below us, but also to shine into us, to highlight any impurities, unnecessary weight or unhealthy habits that might be affecting our flight path.

If we are carrying weight or baggage that does not serve our walk with God, then it will eventually drag us downwards. If we refuse to cast off those weights, we'll find our flapping becomes more and more frenzied, as we try to take over in our own strength.

This is actually an ongoing and cyclical process. Our ability to rise above and find those currents and thermals is entirely dependent on our ability to surrender and subject ourselves to God's purifying methods. We can only 'ascend the hill of the Lord' if we have clean hands and a pure heart (Ps. 24).

Today's devotional is a reminder to form a habit of regularly coming before God, again and again, committed his purification process. Being fully surrendered means that God doesn't have to fight for the glory to go to his name - we have learned to get out of the way. We become a partner that God can really work with. However, we must continually subject ourselves to the process of purification, ready to lay down baggage that accumulates over time, even if we feel like we have done this before!

Take some time today to intentionally give over the baggage you may be carrying, and to assess any habits you've noticed you have, even those that you may have dealt with in the past. Make sure that you're not holding on to anything that may be weighing you down and preventing you from soaring and finding new heights with him.

DAY 29

The strategy

In the morning, LORD, you hear my voice; in the morning I lay my requests before you and wait expectantly.
Psalm 5:3

When it comes to waiting to hear God's voice, we must remember that this is not 'one size fits all'. Some people may have a similar calling to us, but God may give them a completely different strategy. The way that God may have asked one person to go about their tasks may be completely different to someone else. We must be careful to honour the walks of those around us - especially when they are being asked to do something similar to us in a way that we have heard from God NOT to.

In these situations, it is easy to judge and condemn our neighbour, but we have to keep in our minds and hearts that God has made that person a different creation, with different capacities and abilities. He may be teaching them something, or teaching us something, or sparing us BOTH something! We must always act with honour and respect when it comes to the ways that those around us follow God's calling.

God is amazing at giving each of his unique creations a unique strategy to walk the tailor-made path that he has had planned since before time began. Each person's path will be different, and we cannot make presumptions based on our own experiences.

Just as importantly, we must also learn to ask God for the specific strategies that he has for us. We shouldn't assume that the same strategy will work in both a supermarket and a battle zone!

In Numbers 20, Moses learned this lesson the hard way. God asked him to speak to a rock on his journey through the desert, yet he struck it instead. *"But that's what you asked last time!"* you can almost hear him thinking, as he hears that he is no longer allowed to set foot in the Promised Land. Moses found out that God had a different battle plan for a different time and place.

We, too, must discover God's strategy for each individual situation. We are often too quick to assume that one strategy 'fits all', and then wonder why things collapse or don't work out the way we thought they would. This is another opportunity for 'adjusting our posture', which we studied in the *Awakened* devotional. As we soar higher with him, we learn that a different flight pattern, an altered flapping rhythm and a new perspective is needed for each set of currents, landscapes and environments.

Take some time today to consider whether you have judged others for taking a different path, and also to check that you've asked God for the unique strategy he has for you. That's the way to reach the promised land.

SOAR

Day 30

Vision

You prepare a table before me in the presence of my enemies. You anoint my head with oil; my cup overflows. Surely your goodness and love will follow me all the days of my life, and I will dwell in the house of the LORD forever.

Psalm 23: 5-6

Having gone through this *Dare to Ask* adventure, of *Dreaming* again, of being *Awakened* to who he really is, and therefore who we really are, and learning to rise above and *Soar*, it's easy to imagine that we would eventually arrive at a destination of vision, calling and destiny.

But this isn't necessarily the way that God works. Sometimes he does bless us with a vision, a direction; something that he wants us to 'do' in life. But sometimes our calling is simply to live a life surrendered: to acknowledge our passions and dreams, to truly engage with who he is, to trust him, and to walk in blind obedience.

We do not always get the full picture, even though learning to soar should enlarge our picture of what we are called to. What should always happen is that our vision of what God has for those around us expands, and that our dreams and passions and how they can impact ourselves and the world, should grow. We should be able to see great security in our identity, and gain understanding of how we've been made.

If your walk with God has grown, and you've learned more about how you interact with God, he can use that, even if you don't yet have a full vision of his plans for your life. Our vision for this great adventure should be more about understanding the character of God and representing him well than about having a specific task to do. We are often too task-orientated, and I would suggest that until we understand our God-given identity in him, he may be withholding that unique 'to-do' list. The list cannot become what defines us; we can only operate once we know our identity and become entirely wrapped up in who he is.

Be encouraged as you finish this adventure - this is only the beginning! It is an invitation to challenge the way you've been approaching your passions, dreams and understanding of calling. It's an opportunity to flip some thinking patterns on their heads and to look at things from a different angle. It's a chance to reorder your heart, soul and mind so that you can be fully surrendered and truly ascend the hill of the Lord.

Be blessed as you soar on wings as eagles, as you find in him the strength and currents that will sustain you on your journey. Be blessed as you understand more about how your dreams and passions have purpose, and how God created you to think outside of your own experience - because that is where he can be found. Be blessed as you are freshly awakened to who he really is, who he's made you to be, and the unique partnership you can be in with him for the sake of his Kingdom.

Be blessed!

Reviews of Dare to Ask

What you are about to read is like a good movie with various characters, vantage points and visceral moments that are all connected by a common theme – one of great risk and great reward. I think there is something in all of us that wants to believe for great things. *Dare to Ask*, explores that belief by reintroducing a cast of biblical characters whose experiences and decisions clearly correlate with life's challenges and circumstances today.

Like a master archaeologist, Simcha skillfully brushes away the dust and debris that has covered over dormant dreams so that divine destiny can be rediscovered once again – not just the destination, but the process. The revelation in the title chapter alone is well worth the price of admission, but the waves of wisdom, insight, honesty and personal application continue to roll until the very last page.

Dare to Ask challenges the resigned mindset that we are merely silent spectators in this life and beautifully reminds us that dreams are possible, miracles are real and hope is attainable if you just dare to ask.

Steve Carpenter
Founder, Highway 19 Ministries – Jerusalem

~

To the reader of *Dare to Ask*, I would say that when you reach the end of the book, you will conclude that this has been a kairos moment. It is a serendipity, a surprise discovery. Instead of it focusing on aspects of worship from a gifted worship leader, you will be taken on a moving personal journey that deepens your love for the Messiah. It leaves a lot of questions unanswered, but you are left with the deep assurance that the Lord is in control. As readers, we are simply left to keep on asking and keep on trusting. This is a beautiful devotional book written from the heart.

Dr David Elms
International Christian Embassy Jerusalem UK Director

~

Dare To Ask has a beautiful tapestry of practicality and spirituality woven throughout the pages. It challenges readers to dream our God-given dreams, use our God-given gifts, and remove clutter from our hearts so that we can experience the fullness of what God has for us. Through her testimony and scriptural insights, Simcha demonstrates how to be grateful in all things – including trials and desert places. If you need encouragement, restoration or a fresh stirring of hope in your heart, you will find it here! Prepare to go deeper...

Michael & Sara Thorsby
Burn 24-7 New Bern, NC Directors (USA)

Available Now
simchanatan.com

OUT NOW

Printed in Poland
by Amazon Fulfillment
Poland Sp. z o.o., Wrocław

58109944R00047